Axioms

&

Digressions

www.tgrmsk.com

TGRMSK

a spce

Axioms
&
Digressions

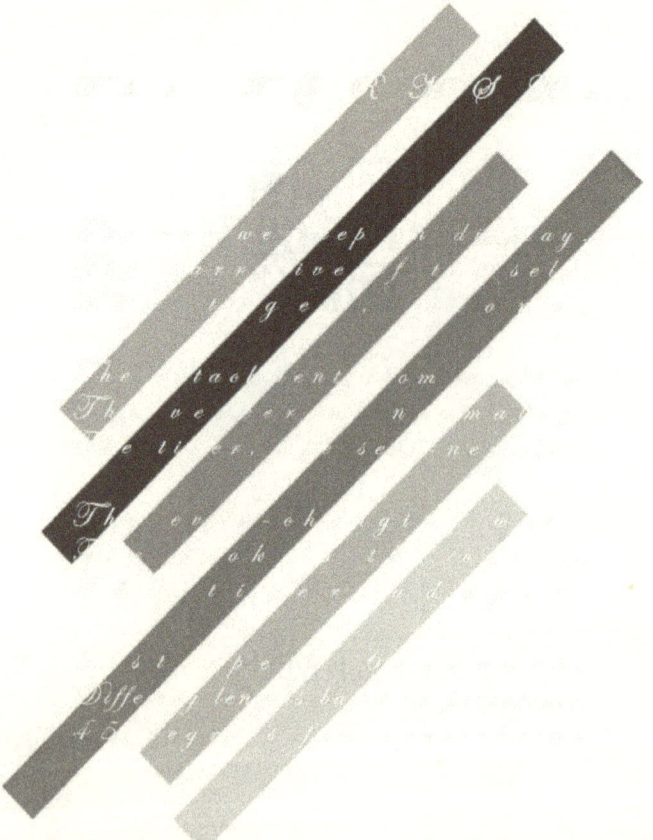

TGRMSK

Copyright © 2017 TGRMSK
All rights reserved.
ISBN: 0648127125
ISBN-13: 978-0-6481271-2-3
ISBN-13: 978-0-6481271-7-8 (ebook)

This book is for:

....

From:

....

Instructions:

Before we start I have to let you in on something; this is not a book. Actually it is, but not in the 'normal' sense of what one would traditionally consider a book. So, some guidance on 'how to read' is necessary.

The Axioms:

Each Axiom is alone on its own page. The Axioms are absolutes and can be pondered, thought about and discussed for as long as needed. As a beginning, one could open to a random page, read the Axiom and stare blankly into space thinking about the Axiom's meanings. One is free to do this as they like, be it in one well-thought out session, or intermittently throughout their days/weeks/months/years.

The blank pages have a twofold reason:
1. To highlight only one Axiom at a time. This way, there are no other distractions.
2. For your own notes, drawings and doodles that you can revisit and rethink.

The Digressions:

These are more topical and opinionated; drawing alternative conclusions to the topics at hand. While still requiring thought, the digressions connect previously unconnected points in a wordier fashion in comparison to the Axioms.

Oh...and that whole *'This book is for'* thing on the previous page:

Is not self-explanatory.

One of the most selfish things one can do is [to do] something nice for someone else. So, the best way to make yourself feel good is to make someone else feel good. You don't necessarily have to give them this book.

One last thing:

You are not allowed to agree with all the content in this book.

You may now begin:

Axiom 001:

The most educated seem to be the least likely to act...except for you of course

Axiom 002:

If all the world's a stage, And all the men and women merely players...then who's watching the show?

Axiom 003:

Dogs that do not have obvious masters are caged & kept detained in institutions; this is called a rescue. Wassup dawg…

Digressions 001:

Bags:

We use them to carry our stuff. This is because society says we need stuff and some of this stuff needs to be with you always, so you need to carry it in your bag.

Imagine we saw bags as just a tool and nothing more we would all be probably walking around with any old carrying implement. I would hazard a guess (because I cannot find a history of the bag) that we would have begun with the old animal skin, so the leather bag is pretty damn old. But let's for hypothesis' sake say that the bag did not evolve more than just a tool, let's say that it was never thought of as a show of status or as a fashion item.

Fast forward to today and I'm thinking that most people would be walking around with plastic bags. It still carries stuff, and we would most likely not be paying thousands of dollars for them, they would most likely be free. And who knows, some clever dick marketer would place ads on the bag and pay people to walk around with them. And so, bag manufacturers, in a bid to outdo each other and provide a better product, would produce better and better bags so marketers can sell them to companies as promotional implements.

Imagine that, a world where you would be paid to carry a (most likely) designer leather high quality bag all because you are advertising the brand (company) emblazoned on it, instead of the other way around.

However, reality is not so sweet, ███████████████ ███████████████████████████████ No, the reality is we pay ludicrous amounts of money to buy…bags. Tools to keep your stuff in. Of course, there's a lot more to it than that, like status and fashion, which leads me to the question:

Given enough time, will all the things we use as tools merely become status displaying, fashion items?

 This doesn't make them better friends, much like the status that brands provide don't make them better tools, but most of us would take them over an unbranded one (if you can find such a thing).

And rightly so.

Axiom 004:

The most difficult thing to tell someone is how humble you are and have them believe it.

Axiom 005:

How easily ignored are facts which antagonize beliefs. How further entrenched are beliefs when antagonized by facts.

Axiom 006:

Industry will sell you the poison, then they will sell you the cure; and you will buy them both.

Axiom 007:

We all live in this world, yet this world is all our own.

Axiom 008:

We blindly argue with others over chickens & eggs the same way we blindly argue with ourselves over understanding & acceptance.

Axiom 009:

One would be naïve to believe a thought as original.

Digressions 002:

Originality:

We all believe we have it to some degree. It's one of the thin veils of positivity that keeps us going. Most times our thoughts are ours alone. For reasons of tact and social acceptance we do not (& should not) express them all. This is all part of being a social creature. Society instils all who partake in it a sense of naivety that leads to a belief that one can have an original thought.

Taking a few gigantic steps back can reveal the exact opposite. To think for a moment or longer, that through the epic span of time & through the mind of every sentient being that has been and is up to this point, that a thought has not yet been thought is well…unthinkable.

Axiom 010:

How can one own something if everything is temporary?

Axiom 011:

Humanity is a mutating dichotomy & it also isn't.

Axiom 012:

The sooner the acceptance of an unfair world, the sooner it will cease to be one.

Axiom 013:

The places and ways things are made become increasingly hidden; as is our interest in them.

Digressions 003:

Health:

Returning from The Summer Palace of the emperor in Beijing we see a man seated on the footpath. A small wooden box sits in front of him, a small piece of paper resting atop the box. Next to the paper is an inkpot, and a brush in his mouth, why? Because this man has no arms and no legs.

He certainly looks down on his luck, perhaps an accident from unsafe factory work practices commonplace to this country, and the no compensation treatment that usually follows these types of accidents. Perhaps he was born without limbs. Perhaps and unimportant.

Contrary to common assumption, he's not begging. Instead, using his mouth to write calligraphy, Chinese characters, on colored paper. He also takes the time to laminate, frame then sell them on the side of the street to those who pass by.

He's not invisible, though many people walk by hoping to appear distracted by something else. He's the type of person I can see from miles away, separated from the crowd, probably the same way everyone else sees him. I always have uneasy feelings when attempting to pass by. Feelings that are usually torn between, 'should I stop and give something?' and 'what is my drop worth in an ocean of unfortunates?'

I certainly didn't need a laminated piece of paper, I just wanted to give him some money for not begging, however I was advised by my wife to honor the man's effort and buy one of the laminated cards. So, I asked her to choose; she chose '**Health**'.

Not *money*, not *success*, not even *happiness*, but **health**. Unbeknownst to her is the extent of her **wisdom**. A subconscious trait embedded in her from childhood. For this I have no end in thanks.

Health is the first and foremost. **Health** is the absolute of absolutes. **Health** is the all-encompassing. **Health**, both physically and mentally, carries on its back all other human factors. As such, neither *happiness*, nor *money*, nor *success* can be achieved and most importantly cannot be truly enjoyed without **health**.

Here's to yours ☺

Digressions 004:

Dignity:

Wow! I heard this word so many times tonight. People, swarms of them, slowly bobbing from left to right foot, dizzied by the skyscrapers of Shanghai, some of the tallest and most ostentatious in the current world.

It is impressive, a testament to man's ingenuity and ego, these phalluses stand erect, every new one outdoing the previous in size, girth & irrelevance. I for one do appreciate such things but am sincerely questioning the need for such immense structures. I guess we as a species know our engineering limitations by now, as in, what we can and cannot currently build with the information we have. So, I wonder if in meetings where such ideas are born and decisions are made whether anyone ever questions the relevancy of such unnecessary endeavors.

An analogy if I could please: I liken the building of these super-skyscrapers to free speech. Bear with me. Everyone has a right to free speech; everyone has a right to say whatever they want, whenever they want to. This has never been in question. However, the question regarding free speech is *should* everyone say whatever they want, whenever they want to? Is it wise for you to say what you're about to say? Are you even wise enough to make such a decision? Probably not.

This is why we have a constant spewing of dumbness from the mouths of multitudes. Oh, and it's why we have skyscrapers, because no one asked, 'should we build it?', probably for fear of being fired, or worse, ostracized.

Love them or not, these buildings are here and not leaving us any time soon. I'm not immune from taking photos of buildings, though, recently I have tried to apply meaning to some shots. There's one in particular, showing the 3 tallest buildings in Shanghai as the main feature, and in the bottom left corner, a hunched over, dirt covered, rag wearing former human. Judging by the sooty grey bristles on its head, we can conclude this person is old, and is dragging behind it nearly worn out sacks filled with plastic bottles which it retrieves from the public rubbish bins. This activity may garner it some money at the recycling plant where it will most likely take these sacks.

Soon after this photo was taken, the former human took a few more steps, stopped, made its way to the handrail and slowly collapsed upon the small step. It turned to reveal a weathered face, and breasts under a char covered t-shirt. It was a she, & she was old & she looked exhausted. This former female human dragging her sacks full of plastic bottles through the searing Shanghai heat was resting her bowed twig legs, her arched back revealing a pronounced hump between her shoulders, quite likely from a life of bent over toil, rice farming perhaps?

Perhaps this government of hers, as it's known for doing, took the multi-generational family owned and run farm away from her to develop another (ghost) city to artificially and temporarily keep the economy afloat. Perhaps and unimportant.

All I can tell you for sure is while this former human slumped motionless against the handrail, many current humans strolled past her casually, wowing at the buildings. One group in particular were a family walking behind us. From their dialect (and attire) it was obvious they were from less sophisticated parts of China. They walked past the former female human and accidentally dropped some paper money, enough to get by for at least a couple of weeks. This money landed right in front of her. Without hesitation, she straightened her head and in a deep husky growl, alerted the family of the money they dropped and to please pick it up.

The family promptly complied, bemused & amused they walked away LOL-ing at an event they can certainly tell their current human friends back in their hometown.

Our former female human returned to her motionless stupor.

Her name is Dignity; she is a former human, free from the ego, free from the possessions that possess current humans. Free from the inhumanity so entrenched in humanity. Just, dignified & free.

Axiom 014:

The idea of nobility in selflessness drowns in irrelevance once you consider the helpless cannot help each other.

Axiom 015:

The extremely wealthy need only thank the extremely poor and the extremely poor need only curse the extremely wealthy.

Axiom 016:

Deserts don't need rain, else they cease to be deserts.

Axiom 017:

Technology advanced faster than wisdom. Hindsight shook its head.

Digressions 005:

Solutions:
Does a solution actually solve a problem? No.
To solve, or dissolve, a problem implies that it ceases to exist. This is a myth, because as long as the solution exists, it means the problem also exists with it. A solution is usually applied on top of a problem and hence why so many of our so-called solutions end up causing other different problems elsewhere.

A real 'solution', for lack of a better word, would be the acknowledgement of the problem and a redesigning of the system that caused it, to prevent it from occurring. This would make a problem disappear. This should also impart on us a certain knowledge we can apply when designing other systems so as to prevent further problems.

While problems still exist, and will continue to be created, we must keep in mind that solutions may most often be the worst problems of all.

Axiom 018:

The thought of making money, once established, encroaches upon all other thoughts, rendering us as one dimensional as the pursuit of money itself.

Axiom 019:

Empathetic grass gets trodden on by the hooves of meritocratic virtues. Would it be unfortunate should you slip and fall off your high horse?

Digressions 006:

Unfortunitis:
Beggars; a guy with half a leg on crutches wearing an eyepatch. He's thin yet his skin droops in piles like an ill-fitting suit. Perhaps evidence of a once rotund figure, in better times, perhaps and unimportant. He is one of the many at the train station entrance. Standing near him a well-intentioned soul collecting donations of money to feed elderly folk. She reminds us that $20 will feed a person for the whole day. This makes us sad considering we've just given them $1.20 and only have $100 bills in our pockets.

This is Hong Kong after all, things move rapidly here, including the people, especially the people, who woosh past these 'blights' on humanity, hoping not to be the subject of their attention. Young or old, male or female, wealthy or working class, these unfortunates remain strangely invisible to all passers-by. It's like they suffer from a disease. I call this disease: Unfortunitis.

This is a strange disease indeed, as it appears to affect the people who don't actually have it. It seems to begin in the corners of the eyes and spreads like a glaze to wipe out the existence of the unfortunate, turning them from a tangible being to nothing more than a wall of uncomfortable goop they must wade through in order to emerge, inhale and continue on their merry way. The feeling of the experience is thusly removed from the brain however, the knowledge and location of the unfortunates remains.

I have one idea on why such a disease exists. Being an unfortunate is no longer a fate handed down from the gods, but something that has happened by your own hand, it is your fault somehow. It's a comforting thought to those of us who have been afforded the continued luxury of being fortunate or won the vagina lottery. Of course, it's our own hard work and perseverance keeping us afloat in this whirlpool of fairness and justice. Those who get sucked to the bottom are simply not swimming hard enough. It's very comforting, it makes us feel less guilt, and that's good because it allows us to pass by and overcome these awkward and uncomfortable moments.

Only but a single thought crosses my mind as I successfully navigate past these unfortunates, closely tailing the person in my front so as not to be subjected to their sad, puppy-eyed gaze. "Heavens forefend any misfortune to come my way, for if this is the mind-state of the majority who claim their success on merit, then my family and I will be right-royally fucked, and so will you and yours" and that would be unfortunate.

Axiom 020:

Your current world is the present version of your past and a clear indication of your future.

Axiom 021:

If one is a product of their environment, then it is the environment that needs tending to rather than the product.

Axiom 022:

If comparisons were done correctly, one would soon find overwhelming similarity and minor difference.

Axiom 023:

You can lead a horse to water but you cannot make it drink. You can lead a human to freedom but you cannot make it think.

Axiom 024:

The tyranny of being one's self does not require election nor coup d'état in order to change regime.

Axiom 025:

Damned is the one who dies from a thousand tiny cuts over a span of time.

Digressions 007:

Erwin's Feline:
The world that holds the hungry
Is the world that bears the obese
The world that coddles the elite
Is the world that shuns the meek
The world that reacts with violence
Is the world that yearns for peace
This world is our forever
This world will one day cease

The world that is all you know
Is the world you know nothing of
The world from which you grow
Is the world you will become
The world that you possess
Is the world in which you're held
This world that feeds our breath
This world will see us felled

The world that paints our calm
Is the world that fuels our rage
The world that stunts our charge
Is the world that turns our page
The world that binds our herd
Is the world that keeps us alone
We all live in this world
Yet this world is all our own

Axiom 026:

"I respect your stupid opinion", said the ego to the world.

Axiom 027:

Of what relevance are the seasons to modern mankind?

Axiom 028:

A piece of shit is not ashamed of itself.

Axiom 029:

Tell people they cannot do something long enough, & soon you will be watching them do it.

Axiom 030:

The best advice is given to yourself.

Axiom 031:

One who acts without regard for nature is a fool.

Axiom 032:

Money is a hammer.

Digressions 008:

The Whatabouts & the Real value of Life:
Is one life worth more than another? Are lives of people equal? Should everyone be treated in the same way? This world and its almost daily calamities force these & other questions upon me. Thanks to an over imposing media I now have no choice but to know about events and causes that not only don't interest me but downright annoy.

It seems when tragedy strikes a first world nation, the whole planet clamors over each other to 'show' support and display the standard veneer of short-lived solidarity before returning to the excruciating purposelessness of their daily minutia. And always amongst the voices of support there is the ever-growing legion of the 'Whatabouts'.

The Whatabouts bring up similar calamities (usually terrorist activities) that happened recently or in some cases regularly in third world or developing nations, always touting the line; "Whatabout the [insert number here] people who were massacred in [insert 3rd world/developing country here]? No one seems to care about them [insert hashtag here e.g. #alllivesmatter]"

While they do have a point, and yes, all lives do matter, however, some lives matter more than others, and the ones that matter most are the lives from first world nations. While it may seem mean to even think such a thought, it's unfortunately true.

This does not concern the reasons why a nation has come to be first world, developing and third world; this concerns the present; the here and now.

So, let's begin with the bottom line. A life from a first world nation is quite likely to earn more income & add more relative value to their country's economy. A 'first worlder' is more likely to have received a higher standard of education; have more disposable income; pursue creative endeavors; have a better understanding of the world; have access to more information; not to mention suffering from first world problems & a whole host of other advantages.

We can also relate to first worlders because they live a similar kind of life. Perhaps they shop at the same brand stores, listen to the same music, eat at the same chain restaurants, have similar laws and political systems, have travelled to the same destinations, work similar, if not, identical jobs & most importantly, have the same fears & anxieties.

Even people in third world & developing nations are more likely to know about the lives of first worlders through TV, radio, internet, press & word of mouth. However, this relationship is non-reciprocal.

But the most important thing, is that a first worlder is more likely to make a considerable impact on the world whether it be for business or philanthropic pursuits BECAUSE they have the tools, the robust institutions & support systems to allow it to happen.

For these reasons, the majority are more likely to subconsciously place a higher value on lives from first world nations.

The Whatabouts are no different. They too subconsciously place higher values on lives of first worlders. However, in a bid to appease ego, they seek out something to 'Whatabout' about, because their voice would be lost if they joined the gigantic crowd showing support to the first world calamity. The Whatabouts are a fundamentally required portion of the population. They are the checks & balances against the tsunami of lemmings who parrot the opinion of the day. The world would indeed be a boring place without the contrarian contributions of the whatabouts; but it's not their existence that irks me. What bugs me is that they're wrong.

When offering the often-ignored news, the whatabouts imply a distinct belief that all lives should be judged and mourned equally. This is not only incorrect; it is grossly negligent because almost all whatabouts are also first worlders.

I would like to strongly reiterate that all lives DO matter, however, the majority shows that lives of first worlders matter a great deal more than the rest of humanity. At this point I would like to also clarify that there is nothing special about first worlders, they do not have higher intelligence, better physical prowess nor a keener sense of enjoyment & appreciation than third world & developing nation people. First worlders are only that because they have won the life lottery of having been in the right place, at the right time.

Axiom 033:

The system to which you're bound for survival is the same one responsible for the demise of others. Now choose!

Digressions 009:

Constantness:
The other day I found a song that I fell in love with, I wanted to hear it over and over again. This feeling reminded me of my teenage years. My love for music has since died down a lot, mostly due to time constraints, but I still love music and this song was really clicking with me; I listened to it for a few days, at least 8 times per day.

So, today I'm not really feeling the song as much. It's not giving me the same energy. I know the song itself hasn't changed, and I know that if I was back in my teen phase I would still be loving this song just as much for at least a few more weeks, or even months, and in some extreme cases, years.

My attention span has waned. This is no surprise and I'm not alone. I call this; Constantness.

The never ending, interconnected, Borg-esque stream of information delivered via every medium & accessible at all times for almost zero cost gives us no chance to reflect on the past nor imagine a future. This constantness makes us lose any points of reference, and without this we lose our place, we lose our sense of purpose, and ultimately our ability to *enjoy* is negatively affected.

And if this is happening to me, what hope is there for my daughters? We are but two mere parents against a societal regime of constantness.

Digressions 010:

Where power lies; realities & myths:
Make a change! Make a difference! BE the change you want to see in the world. We've all seen these and similar memes trolling mostly around the internet. This is the predominant ideology amongst the masses that are growing weary of the system that keeps them as indentured servants. The notion is admirable, that if you want to make a change in this world, you need to begin with yourself. The power of one is nothing, but if a movement gains traction, at the grassroots level, there is a potential to get the attention of the masses and eventually make that change.

However, the reality is quite different. There is almost always a motive behind any campaign for 'systemic change'. These motives are usually varying & ill defined, and in some cases not defined at all, amongst the swarms of active campaigners. These motives & motivations grow as a direct result of the pain points endured by the layman of the day. Each one of these can be different and in many cases directly conflict with each other. As a result, almost all of these movements eventually run out of steam & relevance, affecting nothing other than acting as news fodder for a dilapidated media, sometimes even helping to 'tighten the noose' so to speak of their own necks.

Power to the people! NOT!

Power to the politicians! NOT!

<u>Power to those individuals who were lucky enough to position themselves in places within the systems by which we are governed, where there is a net capital inflow.</u> THIS is where the power lies.

So now that the location of power has been identified, let's move on to see how it can be put to use.

The power to affect real systemic change successfully, within any system, is done in two ways:
1. Make the pain unbearable (enforce a crisis):
   Doing this results in those who are feeling the pain to take actions or ask for others (usually their elected officials) to take actions to 'make the pain go away'. This usually results in further restrictions of freedoms to some degree and in most cases an increase of the initial pain or an increase in the number of pain points.
2. Make small, incremental changes to the system over time:
   This is a very effective & covert way of affecting real change.

To put it bluntly:
- Don't use option 1, why?
- Because using option 2 would require you to position yourself in the current system where there is a net capital inflow (make money)
- Then you make small, incremental changes to the system over time (use money obtained in the above point to buy politicians, lobbyists & lawyers)
- Achieve objective (if you haven't been corrupted by your own self over the time it took you to get the money in the second dot point)

As you can see, in order to affect real systemic change in the world, you need to know where true power lies, how to achieve it, & most importantly, not to get corrupted in the process.

It is this last point of not getting corrupted where many

good folks have failed. So now let's turn our focus towards tools & techniques to help us become less corruptible. I have chosen 2 out of many because it's all that most would need if applied as prescribed. The tools below play on human fallibilities. We know enough to about our-selves to know where we will fail. These tools provide a system to which you are bound and by which you are governed, in order to achieve your objectives.

The best way to avoid corruption is to combine the use of these two tools:
1. A calendar
2. The Odyssean Anchor

Digressions 011:

Death of the 'Teenager' a.k.a. The Immortal Teenager:

The teenager is dead, long live the teenager, albeit 'weekend at Bernies' style.

This needs some explaining...

Most of what we associate with the concept of the teenager can be summed up by these words:
- Independent
- Emotional
- Rebellious
- Adventurous
- Hormonal
- Energetic
- Sexually aware

This phase of human development has been around for many millennia as evidenced by the following quote:

"The children now love luxury. They have bad manners, contempt for authority; they show disrespect for elders and love chatter in place of exercise." - Socrates (circa a long fucking time ago)

However, the actual concept of the teenager as a segment of society didn't come into fruition until after the second world war had ended. This war had delayed a large section of society from making babies when they were more youthful, mainly because they were busy fighting a war, so when the war ended these older boys and girls started fucking. They fucked a lot. They made babies. The babies grew up.

Enter the generation gap; coupled with a shift from a needs-based to a 'desires-based' culture allowed the great youth nations of the time (U.S. & U.K.) to attach an identity (set of common characteristics) to this period of one's life. As a result, this new segment of society created its own lingo, activities, mannerisms & most importantly, wardrobe.

One cannot mention these new 'people' without admitting their wardrobe had a large part to play in forming their identity. Out were the suits, ties and cardigans of the 'cool' set, in were the leather jackets and blue jeans. This is where it gets interesting.

Let's begin with the iconic leather jacket. Worn by aviators and members of the military as functional garb, this item of clothing conjures images of adventure & thrill. Hollywood helped big time to make the leather jacket popular. Movies that were released after the war depicted the war, because it's what the audience could relate to. The heroes, and villains, would no doubt be sporting a leather jacket at some point. Are we making a connection here?

Almost every kid wants to be their parent on a subconscious level but most of them consciously try to be the opposite, and no doubt many of the parents of these new teens had their own leather jackets from their war days which the teen could 'borrow'. The teen however, wanted their own identity, thus altered the leather jacket to adhere to it. Wearing the leather jacket was linking the energetic teen to adventure and thrill, but given there was no more war to wear out the rebellious spirit and energy of the teen, other extra-curricular activities took their place. Activities like listening to rock n roll (black music), talking slang, obsession with fashion, hairstyles, magazines, sex, why? Most likely because their parents didn't like it. They did it all while wearing the leather jacket and whatever else was being adopted.

Later iterations of the teen adopted the blue jeans, but not as they were. You see, *the more people lose touch with what they believe to be their roots, the more they will try to cling to them using all sorts of self-trickery.* Blue jeans were worn by those who worked the land, in a land where work was an honorable activity, especially manual labour. The teens of the time had lost touch with this root because they didn't need it. Industrialisation and advances in technology (thanks to the war) had allowed them to live with so much free time and luxuries, like a disposable income, that a level of subconscious (there's that word again) guilt had set in. Hence the adoption of the blue jeans as another symbol of the rebellious teen. However, blue jeans could not be new looking, that wouldn't be right, so fake wear and tear were applied because those honorable folk who worked the land were not sporting brand new blue jeans. Their jeans were worn out from hard work and so must the teens who wanted the feeling of *'honour via mimicry'*.

The 'teen' had been quickly commoditised by an eager, burgeoning fashion industry. Made to look cool, made something to be admired. Slowly, the wisdom associated with the aged was overlooked in favor of the effervescence of youth, particularly the teen. Children no longer looked up to their uncool parents, instead making the teen the icon of liberation. In reality, their parents were the real liberators. They fought a real oppression of liberties and won, but in order to do so, they had to be organised, disciplined and steadfast in their beliefs. These characteristics, whilst great on a battlefield, did not translate well to raising the first generation of teens. The military regimen did not fit the lifestyle choices of the teen and so as their parents did before them, the teen also fought in liberation, but from their parental oppressors, mostly by purchasing goods which suited their identity. All the while, industry was there to cash in.

We must also mention there were plenty of children in the production line of fashion fodder which ran like a well-oiled machine, or perhaps in modern speak, a quantum processor, so that each successive iteration of the teen had its own look, slang & activities to garner a parent's disdain.

The teen had its time, of course throughout the teenage years, and when that time passed the rebelliousness gave way to adulthood. It was unwritten yet understood that once one grew out of 'that phase', they would settle down and do all the things that were considered the norms of their society for a person their age. The rebels, the hippies, the punks etc, most 'grew up' and became 'normal', taking up the spots in society left vacant by their predecessors thus allowing certain stages of life to be inextricably linked to milestones of status.

By the time one was a certain age it was expected they had completed some level of schooling. For example, by 17-18 it was expected you had finished high school and many were on their way to university for further study and specialisation. Then it was a matter of getting (not finding) the job you had studied (read: trained) for. Your wage would have been enough to support yourself, and a few others, and bills, and a mortgage, and some other shit too, like maybe holidays and a car, you know, life expenses.

It seemed the simple passing of time was certain to provide you with achieving milestones of status.

But something happened...

More accurately, some things happened. These events have led to the demise of the concept of the teen along with its immortality.

You see, for the production line to continue, the previous iteration of teens needed to 'grow up', 'act their age', 'get a haircut' and 'get a real job'. The only way to do this was to have vacancies in the grown-up world to fill and, most importantly, a sense that the future was *gonna be alright*; that if they took this step out of their teen phase, they would experience a real, purpose-filled life.

While there are many factors that contributed to this demise, the main culprit was a decline of the middle class. Stemming from economic policies enacted in the early 1980s, the middle class has been dwindling ever since. As this happened, so too did the catalyst of the ability for the teen to exist; real (non-credit based) disposable income. The facts state the opposite. The charts indicate an almost exponential growth in disposable income levels since after the second world war. Sure, that's probably due to the doubling-down on the desired-based culture of the modern time.

Fake disposable income increased, allowing one to make an easier transition to becoming a teen, but increasingly difficult to move on from being one. The goods the teen spent their cash on were becoming cheaper, more readily available and numerous thanks to cheap overseas labour and an increasingly cunning industry. However, this income was not enough to sustain the transition out of the teen concept. The 'getting a decent job' part was becoming increasingly rare also, due to automation, offshore outsourcing and a general 'putting-off' of retirement by the previous generations who were spooked by economic crises and wanted additional financial security for once they retired (if they did at all).

This means, when a teen is looking to move on and 'grow up' there are less and less opportunities for them to do so. Even the ones who do have the opportunity are turning it down, and why wouldn't they? They have a disposable income enough to cover 'teen' expenses and plenty of stuff to spend it on. Doing that is fun. Growing up is uncertain and unaffordable. Doing that is not fun. So, the fun should never end, because when the fun ends, you die.

Who wants to die?

Probably most teens do, but who can afford to die?

Not many.

So, they must live on. Cursed to walk the earth as teens immortal, and walk they will as tricenarians and a few quadragenarians, dressed in vegan leather jackets and organic denim skinny jeans, to lay a wreath on the grave of the concept of the teen.

'Here lies an idea, buried by the frivolity of its own folly.'

Axiom 034:

As abundance is to scarcity, as is the value of information to wisdom.

Axiom 035:

It sure is funny the things we take seriously.

Axiom 036:

You're not stuck in traffic; you ARE traffic.

Axiom 037:

There are two types of people in this world; you and me.

Axiom 038:

Patience comes to those who wait; Wisdom comes to those who think.

Axiom 039:

The Rat Race: Whether you win or lose, you're still a rat.

Axiom 040:

It's impossible to think outside the box. The box is all you know and as you learn, your box doth grow.

Axiom 041:

Just another brick in the wall, but without one, the wall shall fall.

Axiom 042:

If privacy is a relic, what is the point of fear?

Axiom 043:

The obsession for success leaves succession in a mess.

Axiom 044:

Be Hungry, before you eat.

Axiom 045:

Are you strong? Or are you wrong?

Axiom 046:

Forgive & remember or repeat and regret.

Axiom 047:

The collective sorrows of the people who hope for a peaceful world can know not of any belief, other than in each other as individuals.

Digressions 012:

Leader vs Manager, & the effectiveness of democracy:

What is the point of a democracy if voters are uninformed?
One can safely assume that it boils down to the candidate with the best marketing campaign; and in the politics of fear, the campaign which strikes fear in more people will ultimately win. This is because the informed person who knows all the nuances of policy gets one vote, as does the ignoramus, and their votes are equal.

By that logic and given most people are uninformed (and increasingly misinformed), scaring lots of people to vote for someone so as to put/keep them in power is a democratic function.

It's as though politicians know, that we know, that they are dodgy. So, the marketing is not about how good they are, but how much worse the others are in comparison.

This is a reflection on society, and these politicians are treating nations as though they're running a business, a business in which they are merely managers. Given society values money, businesses make lots of money and CEOs are merely the managers of the business, hence manager equals success.

In this day and age, manager is to success as leader is to risk, and in business, risk is a no-no. It is mitigated & minimised as much as possible. This is the current system, the one that mitigates & minimises leadership as much as possible.

We might say we want leadership, but what we really want is management, because leadership is risk and risk is something we fear. Granted, if our systems are good, effective & fit for purpose, one would only want sound management to keep it ticking along. However, if our systems are not these things, if our systems are failing, one would want a leader. A leader would cause the crisis necessary to change a system, but in the politics of fear we succumb and bring in another manager or worse, an ignoramus.

We seem abundant with managers but bereft of leaders. We can't relate to leaders. We're scared of leaders. They always seem like they're going to shake up the status quo...shame. They seem like fun.

Digressions 013:

Innovation:

Innovation is largely dependent on 3 things:

1. Being an outsider:

Innovation is a word which has become commonplace in our vernacular in recent times and as with many words which once had epic meaning, the prevalence of use of such a word has left it, for the most part, meaningless. Epically meaningless (I couldn't resist).

Innovation, for lack of a better word, has rarely ever come from within the area that was innovated. The Internet came from the military; Refrigeration came from trying to find a prevention for malaria; Computer programming came from the 1890 U.S Census and many more. The point being that the end use of the knowledge emanated from a completely unrelated discipline, conducted by an outsider. Most often this outsider took a piece of knowledge, tweaked it and used it for a completely different purpose.

2. Not being an expert in the field of whatever it is you're trying to innovate:

This outsider has, throughout history, been an amateur. This is generally because experts are, well, experts...but they are experts on things they have proven, they are experts of the past and as such, they are mostly reluctant to experiment, because they've already done that and learnt all they believe they should know, hence why they are experts, not experimenters.

In step the amateurs, who don't know what's going to

happen if they do something, they're still learning and it's in this learning phase when the innovations occur.

3. Being childlike

The curious nature of a child is well-known. Rarely are they cautious, rarely are they bored and rarely do they know what's best for them from an adult point of view. Children are natural innovators.

You would probably not want to stand up and spin around and around as fast as you can right now. Of course not! That shit makes you dizzy and you may fall and smack your head, but kids love doing this. Spinning around and getting dizzy is a child's first high, like a drug high. You may have never thought of it that way, probably because you grew out of it, but you used to think (or not think) like that, you used to act on impulse without knowing, planning and analysing, all of which are the antithesis of innovation.

Axiom 048:

I'm much too wise to be sure of anything I say or do...maybe.

Axiom 049:

Wisdom begets humility though does not contain it.

Digressions 014:

The Abundance of Scarcity:

Scarcity is everywhere! Look around and you'll see. The things that are coveted most are scarce, and this makes them valuable. We value them highly, we covet them as they promise us status, individuality and success, but the abundance of things that are scarce has yet to be realised and we seem to be blind to it.

Driven largely by marketing tactics that understand the animal idea of the fear of missing out also known as FOMO. It has been measured (by actual scientists in lab coats) that the FOMO is 4 times stronger than the joy felt by a person when they win or gain something. Hence it only makes sense to sell something that is hardly available, difficult to obtain and due to its popularity will run out soon.

We fail to see that diamonds are the most common gem grade materials on earth; we fail to see that the 60-year-old woman in a track suit carrying a designer handbag means that handbag is not exclusive; I fail to see that while there were thousands printed, my Michael Jordan rookie basketball card is as valuable as the air I breathe.

This is not a big deal, because FOMO is a key driver of action and a very effective motivator, however, it becomes dangerous when applied to a mindset. A scarce mindset is very much like the 'scarcity ideas' of the products and services we covet, except it is applied to the thoughts in people's minds. This is dangerous because unlike almost everything in the universe, thoughts are inexhaustible.

Scarcity in thoughts drives fear of sharing ideas for fear of not receiving credit and reward. Scarcity in thoughts produces the vocabulary to match and if you're using scarcity derived words you will no doubt convert these words into their relevant actions (or inactions).

In the realm of thoughts, there is the only true abundance. In the realm of thoughts, what is truly scarce is scarcity itself. The failure to realise this, is why we're stupid.

Axiom 050:

When art employs a process, the process becomes the art and the artist merely a tool.

Axiom 051:

Oh, how I long to be mediocre.

Axiom 052:

If one gets drunk from power, they can be sober. Just take care not to stumble, when one is hungover.

Axiom 053:

The comfort of anonymity is a blessing to the thoughtful and an unnoticed waste to the droneful. Both stare in silence.

Axiom 054:

Anyone can turn water into wine, it just takes time.

Axiom 055:

If you're so fucking smart, why are you so fucking poor?

Axiom 056:

R.I.P.
Here lies spontaneity. Buried by the burden of alleged choice.

Axiom 057:

The rain reflects a growing awareness regarding our appearance. As we age our reaction to it changes. The rain remains the same.

Axiom 058:

Once a parent assumes the role, it becomes one for all children.

Axiom 059:

A lynx needs a caterpillar for its survival.

Axiom 060:

Nothing is explained entirely by a single theory...except this one

Digressions 015:

four-oh-four:
we keep serving the servers
react with élan for LAN
get a life high when we find free wi-fi
blow our loads at the speed of downloads

we go loco for media that's social
laugh with glee when we stream for free
in 4k or in the least, HD
we share our maps and bare our snaps
we shut our traps to have our apps

we don't get internet; it gets us into nets
the web is world-wide, but it's more like a herd hide
bits make a megabyte, dimwits think they're mega-right
tits get mega-likes and shit's gettin hella tight

the newsfeed gets fed all the thoughts in your head
you take it to bed like it's the one you wed
don't let up because you're not read up
I guess the feed is not fed up, with you yet

we love to like but don't like to love
we grab the mic but know not what we're speaking of
we check in, but don't check out
we're linked in, to a chain of doubt
although we share and we're aware, it's not like we care
to be fair; we're all in it to win it...so we gotta pin it

tweet tweet, bleat bleat
beat meat, skeet skeet
the ramifications of instant-gramifications

don't rate my status update
criticism is hate

you're a hater, so see you fuckin later
you don't know me or the story I tell
or maybe I don't know myself all that well

what's a vine without grapes?
what's a pin without a point?

what are you without a view?

what's the score?...404

Axiom 061:

What are we but a blink of an eye in the life of a mountain.

Axiom 062:

A day not 'lived' is a day spent in death. Temporary deaths are required for perspective, beware so as not to make them the norm.

Digressions 016:

The Applause:

Hi, my name is TGRMSK and I hate applause...just jokes, I love it!!

It's not that I'm a fan of the sound of people smacking their hands together displacing air etc. It's more about the intent behind the action and sound of the applause. It's an uplifter, a motivator, it's validation, it's a reason to continue doing the things you're doing, to get more applause.

I don't think I'm alone in liking applause. There are plenty of people who love it. We like it when other people like us and approve of us. It sounds very self-centered, but it's quite the opposite and it has me wondering if anyone is actually capable of being self-centered.

One of Shakespeare's most famous speeches from the play 'As you like it' begins with this: 'All the world's a stage, and all the men and women merely players (actors)'. There are multitudes who would agree with this view. So, to question that, an extremely wise man wrote 'If all the world's a stage, and all the men and women merely players, who's watching the show?'

No one and everyone. No one is watching the show for the sake of observation, yet everyone is watching the show to watch others watching them. Most of the time this doesn't even register in our conscious mind, but it is happening, further bolstering my notion that you're not as self-absorbed as you think.

I mean, we tend to think of celebrities as being self-centered, but most of what they do is revolved around getting their audience/fans to pay attention to them, and the audience is only going to do that if they react to the things that the actor says and does.

So then, the celebrity is merely a servant of the idiosyncratic whims of their intended audience. Of course, we'd be generally uncomfortable admitting to this, but any reasonable self-analysis will reveal this as a truth.

So, does this mean the more you like applause, the less self centered you are?

Digressions 017:

The idea of a tomato:

What does a tomato look like?
If you thought of 'round & red' then you would be in agreement with the majority. Great!
But what does it taste like?
Now here's where it starts to get complicated, because if you've grown your own tomatoes, or grew up eating foods that were supplied from non-industrial farms then you would know that tomatoes are quite a flavourful fruit. However, if you've ever bought one from the store, as most of us do at one time or another (unless you have a greenhouse and can grow them all year round), then you would answer one of two ways:
1. It tastes like a tomato, because it is a tomato & this is what tomatoes taste like
2. It tastes vaguely reminiscent of a tomato, bland and watery.

If you lean more towards answer number 2, then you have no doubt tasted a non-industrially grown tomato and therefore have based your answer on a comparison of what you expect a tomato to taste like versus this 'idea' of a tomato that is presented to you in stores. You would have asked yourself 'what is the point of food if it doesn't taste good?'.

Having a reference point is great for comparative decision making, but what if you don't have that reference point?

You answer with number 1. This is what tomatoes taste like because that's what every tomato I've ever eaten tastes (and looks) like. You are unaware of what its actual intention was. You have no reference point. You will not look for alternatives, be them other tomatoes or ways of growing them.

This is representative of so many 'things' (both tangible and intangible) that have, through industrialisation, lost their initial intentions. Through industrialisation, these things have increasingly been hidden from us and, in return, we have lost interest in them as we generally do with things that are in abundance.

Though, we cannot blame industrialisation entirely, as it has given us an abundance of things. This abundance has given us time, lots of it. We have used it to further advance technology. It has been technology that gave us industrialisation which in turn has given us an abundance of bland tomatoes among other useless things. Then it must be technology (not a regression to ye olden times) which will bring back the initial intentions of these things. Via technology, we will return to tomatoes full of flavour, but don't be surprised if you are charged more for them. How perverse...

Axiom 063:

If the nature of nature is naturally natural, then why is the humanity in humans inhumanely inhuman?

Axiom 064:

You can't fight a battle that you know you'll win.

Axiom 065:

Every individual is an exception to every rule.

Digressions 018:

The economics of 'if':

if there were no users
there'd be no pushers
if there were no beggars
we'd all be choosers
if there were no muses
there'd be no art
and if there was no brain
there'd be no heart

if there was not gamble
we'd all have less
because no risk
means no progress
if there were no losers
there'd be no winners
and if there was no fun
there'd be no sinners :)

if there were no answer
we'd have no question
because no life
means no learnt lesson
no. learned. guessing.
words. worth. pressing.
flash of light
idea confessing

if there was no war
there'd be no peace
if there was no cure
there'd be no disease
if there was no I
there'd be no you

and if there was no lie
there'd be no truth

Axiom 066:

The fear of revenge is the greatest stabiliser of society.

Axiom 067:

The masochistic voice of reason knows it's right and so never yells. May very well be the reason why we never hear it.

Axiom 068:

The journey IS the destination.

Axiom 068 & IOU 1:

Now if you'll excuse me, I have to wipe.

www.ingramcontent.com/pod-product-compliance
Lightning Source LLC
Chambersburg PA
CBHW051649040426
42446CB00009B/1049